THE INTERIOR

By Chen Kehua
Translated by Xavier Lin

New York New Century Press Inc.

出 版 人：洪君植

责任编辑：王 渝 严 力

装帧设计：龙雁翎

The Interior

版权所有·翻印必究

出版： 纽约新世纪出版社

New York New Century Press Inc.

印刷：UCHFPQ Inc.

版次：2019 年 09 月纽约第一版；第一次印刷

定价：14.99 美金

国际书号 (ISBN)：978-1-64083-109-4

Chen Kehua
The Poet

Chen Kehua, born in 1961 at Hualien Taiwan, graduated from School of Medicine, Taipei Medical University, and finished his post-doctoral research at Harvard University, U.S.. Presently, Chen is a practicing medical doctor based in the General Veteran Hospital Taipei as the attending ophthalmologist. A virtuoso of poetry decorated with most of the major literary awards and prizes in Chinese literary communities, Chen has also been highly accomplished in other literary genres, having published profusely in fiction, prose, lyrics and plays, as well as poetry. His corpus has been translated into many languages, including English, Japanese, German and more. Quite a number of his poems have been included in the official textbooks for Chinese literature in some Chinese communities around the world. In the past few years, with his creativity venturing beyond literature to conquer more realms such as visual art and installation art, Chen has already put forward exhibitions of his works in these areas on regular basis in galleries and related venues.

Xavier Lin
The Translator

Dr. Xavier Lin (aka Lin Wei-Cheng), acquired his PhD on Translation Studies at Centre for Translation and Comparative Cultural Studies of University of Warwick, UK, is now based at Department of Foreign Languages and Literature, National Chi Nan University, Taiwan. His academic interest focuses on the following topics: the criticism of poetry translation, especially between English and Chinese; the relationship between poetics and poetry translation; the establishment of new criticism frameworks for poetry translation integrating Chinese poetics and Gestalt Theory. He has also been a free-lance translator, published more than thirty translations including works by Kazuo Ishiguro, Juan Ramón Jiménez (from English translation), C. S. Lewis and non-literary books on a wide variety of subjects and disciplines.

After Shedding All the Fetters—
Reading and Rendering Chen Kehua

By Xavier Lin

It has been taken as the default programmed in poetry composition that it is to dance on a tight rope in fetters: joggling many things—prosody, imagery, and myriad of other elements—at once and making an art out of it at the same time. The translator argues that it could be more difficult to dance without any of them—the harder rub to surpass would be to prove the existence of poetry when there is none of these fetters. It is ostensibly the case that one moves freely and easily as a bird fetter-free. How, then, can one prove he is flying—in the sky of poetry?

Poetry readers, especially Chinese speaking readers, have been used to read this genre with the expectation of handling a challenging variety of rhyme scheme, prosody and the intension of unraveling the poetic secret fabricated into the lines. Simply put, it turns out, ironically, that poetry readers wear fetters too watching this show on the tight rope, as in the form of this mentality. As a translator is also a reader, a very deliberate one, this translation offers a different approach. One, the translator hopes, would produce more inspiration and more of and beyond Chen Kehua—a sense of creating poetry in your own being.

How can one describe the poetry in Chen Kehua's poems? The true art of poetry resembles military maneuver, Liu Xie (c. late 5th to early 6th century CE) argued, arguably the greatest literary critic of poetics in Chinese literature. He quoted The Art of War by Sun Wu (c. 6th century BCE), the Aristotle on War in Chinese culture, to explain the secret of poetic art: there is nothing of the infinite versatility in the poetry that cannot be originated through the unpredictably artistic alternation between generality and exception, or between norm and aberration, which can also be the best description of the core of Chen's poetic art.

Famously, Chen Kehua masters in constructing imageries and statements either blindingly vivid or shatteringly provocative or, more than often, BOTH. However, one of the major sources of poetry in his poems comes from the highly significant line break design in each poem— his unique species of power and beauty, one so subtler and more sophisticated as to be absorbed subconsciously, that originates in how the syntax intertwines with the line breaks. A labyrinth of individualistic line breaks; line breaks artistically foregrounding the poetry in each line and creating multiple semiotic systems overlapping the syntax of the text; a text labyrinth seemingly natural but unexpectedly aberrated for the breaks. This, the translator believes, is one of the elements around which the give-and-take translational decision should evolve and that his translator should not ignore.

In any literary work or genre, there are elements that are culture-bound and/or language-bound and need to be adapted, revised or, even, recreated in translation. However, line breaks could transcend or, at least, stay distantly away from these two boundaries and, therefore, render them irrelevant. In other words, it is something unique to each and every individual poet and, even, poem. Chen

Kehua proves a typical example of this situation. This translation aims at preserving this façade of his poetry. To ditch it just for a rendition more transparent in the target language will miss the true poetry in Chen Kehua. If the source poem does not conform to the syntactic convention of the source language on poetic purpose, neither need nor should the target porm conform to that of the target language—uniqueness may appear as an ostensible awkwardness at first sight and poetry is a "strange" way of speaking—said Aristotle.

But of course, there is this issue of how a reader should read freely, without any mental and ideological fetters on the mind and in the heart. After shedding all of the fetters, poetry readers wander like a free Minotaur into the labyrinth of a poem and then another, playing with all the twists and turns architected by the poet and enjoy their own unique journey out and, hopefully—UP.

Contents

Chapter 1 The Interior

003	The Interior
005	The Hanger
006	The Bed
007	The Mailbox
008	The Bonsai
009	The Ballpoint Pen
010	The Bath Room
011	The Toilet
012	The Umbrella
013	The Chair
014	The Window
015	The Ashtray
016	The Telephone
017	The Stairwell
018	The Lamp
019	The Key

Chapter 2 Internet Troops

023	Internet Troops
025	Dusk—A Note from Washington D. C.
026	Tearing the Label 　　—To Allen, on the World AIDS Day
028	The Storm
029	The Line
031	About love
032	And Then I Fell Asleep
034	Shuang Yu (or Bilingual)
036	The Day Started With a 3-in-1 Instant Coffee
037	In Memorial of the Delivery Room of the Ghost Month
039	The Artificial Lake
041	A Billion Names of the Bodhisattva
043	Rainy Days
044	Unrighteous Dog
046	Antonym
048	Upwards Everyday
050	The Chronicle of Mobile
051	Bunches of Thumbs

052	The Insomniac— A micro science fiction/poem
058	The Giant Cat
059	Spilling
060	Group Shot
061	On Selfishness
062	Clothes
064	The Head of Buddha
066	You'd Come
068	The Perfectionist
069	Like Dog Shit, the Death, Under My Sole
071	Why not let the poetry speak for himself?
073	I need a dry man
074	This Life
075	Insomnia
076	In the Rain, What If…
077	Vertigo
078	Paleness
079	One Thousand Kinds of Bird's Songs in the Early Morning
080	Standing Up To
081	The Need
082	Lose Up the Bolt A Bit, Won't You?

Chapter 3 Guide for Garbage Classification

087   Guide for Garbage Classification
089   On the Way to an Art Gallery
091   The Devil in the Room
093   An Open Space in the Woods
095   Agoraphobia
097   The Flower and the Tear and the River
100   Ode to the Muscle
101   Between To Love a Person and to Sex a Person
103   Dawn, Dear Dawn, Please Don't Come
104   The Recipe
106   Meditation
108   Jet Lag
110   The Sage on a Toilet
112   The Fake Antique
113   Animals Come Up To Me
115   The Zoo
117   Wedding Sleepwalking
119   In a Thick Woods—On Effigy Mounts
120   The Rainbow

Chapter 4 Start Reading from the Middle

- 123   Start Reading from the Middle
- 126   The Autumn of New York
- 128   Wide Open
- 129   The Last Grain of Corn in My Dinner Plate
- 130   The Plant Empire
- 135   Beyond the Window
- 137   The Look
- 139   Entering
- 142   Measuring Temperature
- 143   The Wound
- 145   Plastic Flowers
- 147   Will of the Fallen Leaves

- 149   **Chapter 5 Thoughts On Poetry (selected)**

Chapter 1 The Interior

The Interior

It is a hot humid summer dream. From the crowd
Sounds a heated argument about youth.
I zigzag through it
To close the windows one by one—
   lest the body temperature eludes.
You, like a stifling air,
Permeating the June's sky.
The valleys and loins, are scorched by foehn wind.
Watch, the land of Attachment,
For ten, a hundred miles,
Is stretching towards our seeable future
—So I stay steady fast indoors,
Watering the fast-reproducing desire,
And for the imminent drought
Cultivating moisture
And tears—
And I become an unidentifiable plant,

One that should have been replaced long ago,
Unable to assume any mission of beauty, alas!
I live in such a cold room, incubating one
After another hot humid summer dream.
The crowd is whispering a thunder of disillusion.
I walk straight towards you,
Pushing away the less important,
Peeling you open layer by layer like an onion
Until revealing the watery core
—You collapse with a thump.
In fact, around us,
Within the circumference of a hundred miles,
Love and desperation are synonyms.

The Hanger

The shoulders feel the most tired, as many draping
Plump and abundant thoughts,
Like desire, like out-turned pockets
(proven emptied),
Cannot but hang embarrassedly on the outside.

However, the most tired are the shoulders,
For what needs to be upraised at once
Are the head that wants to fly and the rough,
   hairy penis.
When the clothes are taken off,
They become weighty.

The Bed

Two dreams are placed as pair. Saturated and neat,
Far apart,
Out of each other's way.

They are messed up once every night.
   Two heads are placed as pair,
Without asking
Where the sperm and tears shed
Have gone to——every night
They both dream of a ripe pink womb,
Where the egg and sperms
Are stranded quietly.

The Mailbox

My glance is about to shoot through him,
　　full of doubts
And hopes
(self-contradictorily)
After the hand in green sleeve
Touches my name.

I shoot through him; some messages suddenly
Burst
From the floating cube
Into innumerous snow-white confetti,
　　like snowflakes,
Covering all of the lonely wintry hearts in town.

The Bonsai

A bonsai sits on a grayish window sill;
It keeps a small patch of cloud:
Mountain and water; imagine
   an immortal living therein.
Who knows?

The dark green bonsai
Sits on the sill of every window in a city
   that cannot dream.
In average, a person
Owns ten windows,

Yet everywhere looks just grayish.

The Ballpoint Pen

Making even a dragonfly dizzy, this sixth finger
Stands tilting on the pristine
Paper of thoughts.

Swirling and twirling,
Like the paddlers of a helicopter
That cannot take off, it rovers around the thumb,
Unable to elevate the thoughts
   to the heights of the spirit—
Anguish, helpless
And eventually, destined to fall off the desktop.

The Bath Room

Following the procedure,
He takes off the tie, the ring, the denture
The glasses, the credit card,
And the condom, until he is completely
Transparent,

Through and through. In the mirror, he becomes
Completely tender,
      melioristic,
Unable to argue neither
To erect.

The Toilet

Human beings have not evolved
   to perfection yet. Proof one:
The toilet's
Awkward shape.
Which leaves the buttocks hanging supportless
   for a long long time,

The eyes wandering,
The thoughts struggling to elevate themselves
To the height of the altitude of social pages:
Dregs, dregs, dregs, dregs, dregs, dregs, dregs.

The Umbrella

Soaked through with rain
Left forgotten behind the door, resignedly,
Languidly,

Has come.

The Chair

The knees bend vertically.
Who says one needs to stand straight
   to have a view?
The sofa, in the texture of clouds
    And the entrapment of the oil painting,
Is built in big bulges of
Dreams.

A barrette, a cane,
Some etiquette, dignity,
And a moustache. Sitting down,
A man needs only
A chair,
No more.
(lying down, if the shirt is not pleated,
A woman)

The Window

The air conditioning is on. A pale kind of emotion
Recycles in a sealed space,
    recycling   recycling
        recycling,
Unable to dissipate or dilute….

I open the window and shout.
The whole building, like the leaves of lung,
Suddenly collapses.

The world loses its voice.

The Ashtray

Caught in a bowl made of both hands,
　　the dandruff of thoughts.
A garnet smolder
Flares time and again along with the inhalation.

Afterwards, squashed heavily to extinct,
Just like coming on a certain patch of skin.
A sadistic
Metallic orgasm
Is piling up like tattoos, overflowing.

The Telephone

A banana split: for three minutes,
We're nibbling at the phone
From both ends, as if competing
To finish it
First.

"You said you stopped loving me
 but could love really be stopped?"
"I never said I stopped loving you;
 one needs no word to stop loving."

The Stairwell

A vertical passage. Everyone goes up
   and down through here,
Leaving behind muddy shoe prints, smell
And echoes.

"I have lived so thoroughly and solidly."
Have lived;
Lived;
Alive;
Been there.
This is what Heaven hears.

The Lamp

A prompt fruit, grown indoors
On a vertical stem,
Radiating white rays.

If it has been the invisible earth
Watered with electricity
That brought us the civilization of brightness,
And thus nurturing many heads closing up under the light,
    Many nights of crystal, all-night deliberation,
    Many foreheads mirroring each other—
And many evolutions of the mind
    in ultra-high speed, Aye,
I am deeply grateful for it.

The Key

"A bunch of" means I have quite a few locks.
Many spaces stay adjacent but independent.
Pushing in through this, comes
A figure slightly conforms to what I remember;

"What? You've got my key?"
Of course, have you forgotten it?
There was a lover who came and went freely,
More mysterious than the truth,
Simpler than a dream—
Between in and out
He offered secrets as gifts.

Chapter 2 Internet Troops

Internet Troops

To be honest,
We are the Red Guards on the internet, breeding
Lies

And rumors,
Battling against enemies in mask—
Since they sniffed the smell of power
As elusive as the internet

And equally ubiquitous,
It has become verisimilitudinous. They

Burn, kill, kidnap and rob,
Raping the wife of the Truth,

Masturbating with keyboard and mouse,
Always facing toward a certain

Chairman X

And coming.

Dusk
—A Note from Washington D. C.

The dusk lingers in Washington D. C.
   a bit longer today.
The glass curtain skyscrapers line up
Like rows of dominos in surgical precision.

Like towering medals,
They emit, before falling asleep,
Dark brown metallic luster.

Tearing the Label
—To Allen, on the World AIDS Day

We have been so obsessed with
   playing the labeling game that
We fail to realize how afraid of it
We are: "The greatest enemy is Vanity…." And,
Aids is the best tester
For the issue of labeling, for fear
And for how we live vainly.
Illness is a dojo and watching the others
   getting sick is
The regimen. We finally realize
How to dine with neighbors
   and brothers and next table diners
Who are inflicted with Aids,
Eating at the same table, drinking from
   the same cups for decades.
Served to us is
A cup brimming with bitter juice.

   We beg to keep it,
Or else we will never learn
   how to remove the label,
How to test whether love is true or false,
How to see in every body,
   which cannot but decay,
God.

The Storm

In the storm, I watch a round hole on the ground;
Arrays and arrays, aroused by rain,
Of muddy tiny soldiers,

Which forms a whirlpool, heading
Nonstop down towards the eye

Like an expanding typhoon,
Like a vanishing galaxy,
Where I and the myriad
Of things in the storm,

Are trapped.

The Line

Is it real as they say that there is a line?
It divides the two Koreas, the two Germanies,
  the two Vietnams;
There are one even in the middle of Taiwan Strait
And countless lines as border for countries,
  provinces, cities…

I come to the line eventually, when
It is miserably gray,
And, trees have grown into forests.
In the distance, there are one or few bricks
  and tiles falling
And a few vague but very poetic scribbles
  on the wall;
Some endangered animals have moved in;
"Like a haunted town…" a human voice
  rings from afar.

The clearest line should be this one:
    Besides a slightly raised anonymous tomb,
Right beneath my feet,
Where the pasture and the path meets,
The tearing pain we share—

Human beings, walking as if drunk,
    can only follow this line,
One moment towards life;
The next towards death;

In most of the time, they're like me,
Walking and looking towards both ways at a loss.

About love

You walk toward me and
Stop at the same corner.

I've never felt so shiny,
Realizing I am a yellow traffic light

At which you can stop or

Pass by.

And Then I Fell Asleep

And then I fell asleep. I slept between one sentence
And another;
Some dictions fermented in the guts,
Some between the spine and bladder,
Swelling, or growing thorns.

Sometimes, an old man who frequented my dreams
Would smear his features while
Turning the pages for me. But,
I seemed to wake up at
A page randomly turned to—

It was a page either read, or so I thought, and
forgotten or never been read yet;
The page, like an old city,
Was suddenly mapped fresh new today.
I was determined to take a totally

different route home.

I expected to meet a pedestrian
And to recognize him before he me
While we kept our cold politeness
And both slowed down our paces,

As if it occurred to me at the end of a movie
Which I realized then I had seen it—I
Always started reading from the middle
And kept it completely secret from him,

Without revealing even the slightest clue
Or the ending.

Shuang Yu (or Bilingual)

Having one more tongue
Than the mother,
The child speaks fluent Chinese, for example:
Wo you liangtiao shetou (or I have two tongues).

"Zhe shi shuangying jumian"
    (or it's a win-win situation), you say,
"Meitiao shetou dou ying" (or every tongue wins).
In this world where someone must lose
    when someone else wins,
You want to win on a fine spring morning also.

You hear a thousand kinds of birds
    singing outsides,
Unable to treat it as one kind of sound.

"Su—su, su—su," (or lose-lose, lose-lose),

you can't help identify
One of the bird's songs:

Su—su, su—su.

Meitiao shetou dou su (or every tongue loses).

The Day Started With a 3-in-1 Instant Coffee

Punctually showing up in front of the Xerox,
   he is copying the sunlight of 9:01:
     "…or copying possibly any day in life…"

Then, he recopies it,
And recopies and recopies it

Until everything turns completely blurred
Giving the taste of the canned
   3-in-1 instant coffee…

In Memorial of the Delivery Room of the Ghost Month

I, I do not particularly desire watching
The coitus between men and women,
Including pornography; but, the Buddhist masters
Say that is how we reincarnate: We peep at
Our parents making love

When we possess the sperm that enters
   the egg in orgasm
And acquire the flesh-and-bone body,
Feasting on father's essence and mother's blood
And, finally, owning the ticket for entering
   the mundane world;

And then, we fake howling,
While we are, in fact, grinning insidiously

As we glide down out of the slimy birth canal

With the families of the parents closing in, smiling,

Then realizing that the mundane world is full of fools and nuts—can't these people,

Can't they—can't they see
I'm a diabolic ghost?

Note: In Chinese culture, the fifteenth day of the seventh month of the lunar calendar is called the Ghost Day and the seventh month in general is regarded as the Ghost Month, in which ghosts and spirits, including those of the deceased ancestors, come out from the lower realm.

The Artificial Lake

On the last day of a long weekend, when the sun started to set, he rode me on a motorcycle heading towards a rather remote suburban lake in hills. It's artificial, he said. I crouched behind him, wondering in the coldness all the way: Are we really going? It seemed that it was getting dark and we had started long ago, still circling in the block labyrinth of the city. Was it excavated artificially? I thought of a poem years ago: There was a lake outside the house, an artificial one. I asked him: why are you lying here in such a vast and deserted place. The lake answered: "Because this is the only way for God to see me." A drop of tear on the surface of the earth. When we got there, it was not much larger than a drop of tear but hardly deserted. The water was tolerantly clean, the waterside lawn fresh; and the ripples sparkled with schools of tiny fish peeping out here and there. Walking around the lake and leaving, we somehow stopped for coffee at one of the coffee stands on the lake side. It occurred to us that we had rode past a deserted house on the way here and spotted two youngsters spay-painting the outer walls. The paintings were just messy but their eyes were glowing. We imagined that it would have been admiring their works, instead of looking over a drop of tear, that God would choose to do as a pastime on the last day of a terribly boring long weekend. It was getting dark fast. We took the same way back down and there was no light on the way.

A Billion Names of the Bodhisattva

"When lamas write all of the one billion names
 of the Bodhisattva, this world will fall
 into destruction....,"

Rinpoche, into my ear,
Whispers. I cannot help feeling anxious, finding
Everything around me
Begins to show distinct signs
 of deterioration already.

The flowers on the top of Deva wither and fall;
Foul smell floats from the armpits.
The sky, like a faded lens,
Is covered with countless scars by airplanes;
The sea turns into a rancid porridge
With ships like swarms of drowning flies—

"That is merely the projection of the inner fear,"
   Rinpoche
Offers me fake comfort: By then,
   everything will stay as always.

Your life and living, bank account,
   beloved car and lover,
Sex and food—
All there.

However, when you look up into the firmament
There'd never be any star in the night sky,
   not even one.

Rainy Days

On rainy days, a lot of raindrops
Come to window sills for shield.

Their transparent bellies stick flat on the pane
Like sticky little worms trying to
   live there, to rest—

When more and more raindrops come to the refuge
One over another and another,

They merge into each other,
Becoming a bigger drop till.

They become so weighty that
They slide down, leaving trails of tear behind.

"It's all the fault of gravity…"
I close the window tighter.

Unrighteous Dog

I took him to see the vet. In yesterday's revisit,
The diagnose was issued: a deformed value.
I read the list:

1. Gluttony. 2. Loving eating.
3. Always looking for food.
4. Eating anything, whatever can be swallowed.

Depressed, I took him home.
The vet held that, as eating was the first
    and utmost task of life,
There was no need to cure it neither cure for it.

Struck by the issue of soul,
I think of my recently deceased father;
They were once as close as form and shadow—
    Does a dog

Have a soul? Now,
He lies leaning on my calf,
Looking emotionless and relaxed,
Completely ignorant about the fact that
    the person walking him has been different…

But, in the next minute, pricking up the ears alertly
As if there appears not far away
A bitch in heat

Or a bag, smelling like corpse,

Of garbage.

Antonym

We often use the antonym
To understand a word, don't we?
   "Love," for example,
Can only be understood

Through indifference, hatred,
   the farthest distance in the world,
Apathy,
And to stop loving.
The pyramid of the antonym of life,

We build it brick by brick,
This so-called the milestone monument of being

In the endless desert where love has been extinct.
Mobilizing in the name of love,
   one can easily capture

Innumerable eager
Servile hearts…

Upwards Everyday

They all say tomorrow will be better—
    good news!
Here comes the good news:
Tomorrow has taken over the place on the earth
Where human beings occupied
Relentlessly.
And us, we can only go on
    being classified as "today"
And be left with a pile of scraps or defectives
In the depth of the same drawer, unreachable by
The beautiful working sound
    of the machine of Hope—
One day, on waking up,
One'll find the original tomorrow
    has become the yesterday
And there is still a new tomorrow
Taking up that space,

Continuing the exertion

To move upwards everyday.

The Chronicle of Mobile

We have come to an age
When we use the model number of a mobile
To number the year, and,
With the problems caused by the mobile,
To chronicle:

Radiation. Inflammation. Explosion.
   Leakage of personal data.

Bunches of Thumbs

In your cell phone lives a wounded child,
Whose hand is holding a wounded cell phone,

In which lives another wounded child,
Whose hand is holding another
   wounded cell phone...

They text each other,
Clicking thumbs-up.

Whenever you try to turn off your cell phone,
They gang up and attack you:

Why didn't you click "thumbs-up"?

The Insomniac
——A micro science fiction/poem

Over there was the person
   whose sleep was stolen, along with
His dreams. He reported to the Lost and Found
Where there were too many lost sleeps
   to be claimed.
He could not recognize his.
"Each sleep has its distinct texture,
   color or pattern…"
As he failed to find his—"Sorry,
I must have fallen asleep." Then
He walked into the headquarter of the Capsule,
Getting some pills that helped him sleep.
In sleep, he encountered his former Sleep,
Gently held him and cried.
But, in no time, he realized that
   this long-parted sleep was a fake,
A clone almost too real to tell: "you, you,

  you are not

My Sleep…." He blurted,

Shouting, howling: "What did you

  come to me for?"

"I have no idea why I appear here!"

Sleep said, "It's your capsule; it summoned me…

You can summon me any time,

Like turning on a TV

Or your iPhone—

Millions of doubles of me,

At your service any time…"

  He woke from the nightmare,

But the dream, like invisible salt,

Blended into his bland days.

He and millions of other insomniacs,

Entering and leaving the Capsule Tower.

He came to recognize each capsule's texture,

  color and pattern,

Each sleep clone's personality,

  expression, body odor,

And the feeling of holding them.

"I didn't realize sleeps come in such variety…"

    He thought to himself excitedly,
And secretly expected such encounter
    in more strange dreams
Each night when he went to bed on time—
And completely forgot about
    the original sleep of his.
Looking into the mirror, he saw no one there,
"Have I turned into a vampire or something?"
    He wondered, touching the glass,
Which felt like touching the cold smooth
    lower ab of each sleep clone.
"My sleep must have his own looks;
I never recognized it. That's all!"
—When he woke from another and
    yet another strange sleep,
Like waking in the arms of another and
    yet another stranger
With self-loathing disgust,
Starting a day like one in a prostitute's life,
He realized afresh he was a person
    who lost his sleep,
Or, even worse, maybe,

He was still in his original sleep after all,
And, This Life Is Like A Dream.
"Wrong!" he was struck by an epiphany,
    "This life IS a dream!"
So, he (and millions of other insomniacs)
    was in the original sleep after all, and of course
They could not sleep into that sleep but
To resort to a capsuled sleep to embrace the sleep
—He rushed excitedly into the Capsule Tower
    and declared:
I Found The Truth!
The receptionist in the lobby was shocked
    and the guards, grim.
"We still live in yesterday's dream
    without waking up…," he
Shouted to other insomniacs:
"Only when we wake up can we go on sleeping…"
(Only When We Wake Up,
Can We Go On Sleeping)
Then, he suddenly fell into coma, a kind of sleep,
He had never experienced,
    a deep and thoroughly new type of sleep.

A completely strange sleep clone
Opened the door to the room, walking in,
Stroking his hair, kissing him, waking him:
"Are you up now? You've been ill for so long…"
    He looked at the brand new face of the sleep,
Like seeing the latest model of clone
And failing to find any flaw,
A perfect lover: tall, handsome, and deeply in love,
Which made him wonder—can it be so good
    and still true; then he heard:
"Knocked unconscious, you've slept for so long;
    the heads of the laboratory tried to infiltrate
    your consciousness to wake you…"
Was this a dream? If yes,
In which sleep? If not,
From which did I wake up?
And who summoned this sleep?
"Come," the sleep clone said,
    "You must come with me.
Only so,
Can you truly wake up,
Can you continue to sleep."

How familiar, these words! He couldn't help
Walk hand in hand with the sleep clone,
Leaving the room.
Out there, there was only light
And all the sleep clones, greeting him
Like meeting the deceased families;
They embraced each other, greeted,
   and shed tears of joy,
"Where is it here?" he asked.
"The space does not matter here."
"When is it now?"
"The time neither."
"Why am I here?"
"Reasons matter even less here."

Only light,
Nothing but light.

The Giant Cat

The turf of the cat kept expanding
And, finally, encompassed the whole Earth. Often,
It left without goodbye.
Along the remote coastlines, appeared sporadically
In the slit pupils
Nostalgia in the blue of abyssal algae—then

As if spotting a mouse, she
Found human beings—
Seizing in one fell swoop

The tails they had failed to hide away in time.

Spilling

The spilled ink on the desk
Is part of a memory from long time ago—

But the cobweb of the black highways
Still goes on to spread,
Invading virgin land like pure white paper.

Stationery is islands; pens, boats; books, cliffs;
Keyboards, neatly furrowed fields.

The writing that stopped abruptly yesterday
Hid into the pitch dark screen…..

I roll myself up into a ball
Stained with the black.

Group Shot

Then sitting in a row or
Standing together,
They shot a huge group shot. Said: Cheeeeze.

Later,
He examined these pictures several times,
Trying to find, between the smiles,
If there was any connection
Or, between expressions, any kinship—

But, all he could recognize was his own eyes,
Looking towards what none other could see,

A certain mysterious horizon.

On Selfishness

Today, our topic is selfishness. Each of us
Occupies a corner of the conference table,
Deep in thoughts,
Like playing transparent poker cards—
But we can only see through our ourselves.
The transparent cards get strewn on the table—like
Our rambling thoughts; whenever we
Try to focus, we feel distinctly
We are more selfish than the others,
Secretively giving the lousy ones back
   onto the table: "The best
We can do as ourselves
Is only
To trade off on every issue." Until
Every single one of us
Acquires a hand of great cards.

Clothes

Although we have already been unable to imagine
What if, in the human civilization,
There were no clothes, although
We keep praising the fur and feather of
   other creatures,

Although we are one of them—
We have long been tamed by clothes
And praise them servilely in return.

However, some bodies are born natural traitors.
Even when they are perfectly dressed,
You can still see the form and angle of the penis,
The form of the breasts.

Their spines still end with tails;
Their blade bones extend into wings;

At the edge of their cheeks, gills are lurking.

They are really,
Really living here on the Earth.

The Head of Buddha

All of the objects are misplaced. I and
These milestones of the human civilization
Meet in the museum, as if I
Were a little school boy going into
   a wrong classroom.

Surrounded by one after another
   strange yet familiar face,
I come before that of Buddha.
   Time stares at me with eyes wide open
While Buddha looks down low.
He is above and beyond Time—

The bizarre hat I pass by should be
Worn by some brown, huge-breasted woman
And the serpentine sword, held by a bloody hand,
And the belt profusely bejeweled,

belonging to a hero—

I go through one and another room
    experiencing déjà vu,
But am sure none is my classroom.
All the of the objects are misplaced:
A pre-historical flute behind the glass pane

Calls to me, my lips and fingers and lungs;
The spirit of music and dance overwhelms
    me like sunami and meteor showers,

While the head of the Budhisattva
Calls to his body.

You'd Come

Carrying
The three nails you clipped from
   the left hand of the dead
And the three coins mysteriously
   showing up in your pocket
On your twentieth birthday,
The first hair of
The first person who said to you "I love you,"
A tea spoon of the saliva of your lost pet,
And a small piece of shadow your eyelash
   cast on a total lunar eclipse—

Outside your house,
To the corner where you once dozed off,

On the moment the daytime moon
   and the setting sun coexisted,

You would come. You

Would really come before me.

The Perfectionist

What a pity, you are already
Perfect.
There is no embellishment ... possible.

Your A+++++++ and +
Like endless Legoes piling up...

Haven't you notice
The buildings in the Hell

Are eternally so perfect?

Like Dog Shit, the Death, Under My Sole

I walked through a park after rain on a gloomy day
When suddenly my right sole slide a bit,
As if I had stepped on a piece of dog shit
Or a puddle of vomit
Or some kind of a small animal dead
For some time, a decomposing corpse—

There was a very curious kind of slipperiness—
   in the dark.
I kept on walking,
Sensing there on the sole unidentifiable
   strangeness still clinging there:
Is it phlegm, a lump of gum, or a banana peel?

Then I stepped past pavement tiles,
Cement stairs, asphalt paths, iron sewer lids,
Subway platform and the floor in the car—all

strewn with dirty water
And endless footprints from innumerous strangers,
   layers upon layers.

The feeling dogged me till I
   reached my front door,
And, laying my right foot on the thick door matt,
I scraped it a bit.

(Can't help turning the sole upward to check)
I thought this at least
Would keep the death
Outsides for a while.

Why not let the poetry speak for himself?

Poetry always sits in the corner by himself:
    Hair unkempt,
Clothes untidy,
Expressionless and yet heavily occupied.

In today's meeting, there are guests
    speaking all kinds of languages
And fans speaking all kinds of languages,
And also reporters and editors.

Turning on the microphone,
    Language suddenly feels short of words:
"Well, the subject today…blah, blah, blah….
Well, is poetry … and about poetry, blah, blah…"

Responses gushing from audience on the floor,
    hands flying high:

Blah, blah, poetry is… and about poetry,
    blah, blah, blah…
Blah, blah, blah.

Suddenly, words are exhausted.
Everybody looks down to search
In their pockets and finds therein only blah,
    blah, blah…

Meanwhile,
Poetry himself
Ascends onto the stage alone.

I need a dry man

I,
I need
A dry man. On rainy days
My joints can foresee the coming floods.
As moss grows on the eyelashes and
   under the armpits,
It's time when I know perfectly
What I need is a dry man—
Like a pack of desiccant
Tugged away somewhere
   in my humid soul capsule.
How prone it is for my opened body
To get humid and moldy:
"You might as well feast upon me right away…"
Finish it, and,
Along with the desiccant,
Trash it.

This Life

This Life
I see you clearly walking towards me from the last
And then into my next
And into the next of the next,

However, what I have is the present. Whenever I
Wake up dreamless,
I would be concerned I have eternally missed,
Missed you, alas——

I want to return to the moment
   when the mistake happened
To freeze that scene,
Stopping the time:
You'd always be in the position
   of standing up to leave;
I'd always be reaching towards you.

Insomnia

The whole night, through and through,
An insomniac captain
Trots up and down upstairs,
His golden left foot
Knocking in the beat of a heart:

"It's a ghost who hasn't quit hunting yet…"
In the depth of the ocean of my consciousness,
A Moby Dick,
Dream-like,
Is playing carefree.

In the Rain, What If…

From now on, I try as much as I can not to
    look at the eye.
Many a rain-soaked soul is refused the entrance;
The earth is cleaning vigorously
    the evidence of tears—
Alas, the rain. Some people are kissing
    with a glass between them,
Leaving sweat, stains of lips and palms,
    blurred……

I start to wonder how to penetrate or sabotage
This city that glows suddenly, if
I promise to return a piece of lego
If the tower of your dream still needs one.

Vertigo

On-going is my vision
To spin, with me as the center, to the left,
Crumbling block by block, disintegrating,
    and, to the side that cannot poetry,
Fleeting.

I fall anti-clockwise
And run into Time—
A still ksana, I am sure:
The world, after a ksana of madness, swiftly
Recovers. (Alas, in madness so hard to discern)
And the vertigo I suffer
Is exactly the tiny bit of the proof.

Paleness

I would only dare to sketch you
    with a pencil, a 6A,
On paper most resistant to wrinkling.
Because only the unique paleness
Of yours
Corresponds to the long lasting
And
Nothingness
Of the memory.

One Thousand Kinds of Bird's Songs in the Early Morning

In the one thousand kinds of bird's songs
   in the early morning,
I am certain there is an unrecognizable calling
Trying to wake my
Yearning and tumbling soul.

A light like a straw stirs the thin night;
The dream turns and falls heavily on the other side.
Right at the moment when the bird songs fade away,
The sunlight happens to cook well done,
In the nest of inspiration,   one
Unwilling to hatch
And overly proud egg.

Standing Up To

Do you think you only need to hold on
    to your own grief
And it'd be enough for standing up
    to the whole world? Alas,
Perhaps a blade of grass would see more clearly
The wall once built with Mozart or Dostoyevsky
Cannot withstand one aftershock
Of a glance or
One masturbation.

The Need

Right in the short severe coldness of December
One can often feel a crystal
Need to be loved, to be
Deeply embraced, to be
Torn open dissected penetrated
   twisted sucked tramped disintegrated
Breathed slept
Dreamed (or waken),
And then stare

Into the vast barren green in each other's eyes,
Seeing the need.

Lose Up the Bolt A Bit, Won't You?

Staring long and hard at the world's eye
I sometimes feel the sight blurred;
    with the focus pushed
Forward, there's the God;
Backwards, there're ghosts, all kinds of
    heavens and hells crammed together.

Like all kinds of amusement facilities
    implemented in a theme park—
They are all called "emotion,"
    "emotion," "emotion."

The cart named The Mortal World
    rushes up and plunges,
Through cycles after cycles after cycles.

The waiting human beings has formed

a long queue, but suddenly
You, stuck in the line, decide

This time you want to make a splash—
like a blue collar worker.
You, grabbing a screw driver,
Climb up the roller coaster—

(You look like a little screw from behind)

Yap, you are looking for something
to loosen up just a little bit,
Something,
Such as a tiny little screw.

Chapter 3 Guide for Garbage Classification

Guide for Garbage Classification

Monday. We collect the inflammable, the decomposable, but not those that are both nor neither.

Tuesday. We collect those with texts; but, not those with incomprehensible texts nor those with words that can be pronounced in two (or more) ways.

Wednesday. If it is rainy, we collect garbage that is soluble or floats and flows away when littered on water (as into a toilet or a pond in a park). If it is sunny, we collect garbage that you want to keep out of sight the most. However, the size must not be smaller than a music box or larger than a refrigerator that can contain a dead body.

Thursday. We only collect objects that are still

shivering subtly, except those that will sound when crashed.

Friday. We collect objects which we cannot call the name of, cannot give a name to, there is no name for, or everyone has a different name to call.

Saturday. We rest. If you (male or female) book on internet, we will offer special service, but only for those stained with blood or cum, crumbling from a larger object, gnawed by animals, or ended outside the can after you aimed at and threw towards it.

Sunday. We collect all those objects not stated above, except those you have already disposed of from Monday to Friday or those from those who never dispose of any garbage.

P.S. The classification above is not valid on a national holiday; but, based on Labor Standards Law, we collect all of the exceptions.

On the Way to an Art Gallery

They say it is the sanctuary of art, whose collection
   includes the most inspiring works
     of art in the world. The must-see's
       for the tourists of this city.
Though I started out as early as possible, the map
   I had happened to be one failing to
     provide a clear direction of it.
Pausing endlessly to check and making numerous
   wrong turns, I finally came to a
     promising crossroad, deciding to take a break
       for breakfast in the deli nearby
         and, conveniently, to ask for direction.
The clerk, at a lost, said he seemed to have
   heard of it but was unsure.
He suggested I ask at the next block.
Proceeding for a while, I saw a girl with a
   staff ID around the neck and rushed up to

           her for information. She nimbly fished out
              her mobile and clicked the keys as
                 fast as lightening, telling me: It's close.
                 Three minutes' walk away.
Pointing first to the east and then to the west,
   she apologized: Should be this way. Yap.
I resumed my odyssey.
The street became deserted and there showed up
   a homeless holding some cards.
I stopped and looked at him eye to eye,
   not meaning, though, to enquire.
He looked at me and it dawned on me right away:
   All he cared for was food.
I moved on.
It suddenly occurred to me: I could be
   the only person in the whole wide world
      this morning who needed art.

The Devil in the Room

The door opens quietly
As if a cat walks in
Silently, softly even,
Or, carrying in the mouth a piece of sunlight

Murdered. But I did close the door just now,
   I am sure of it.
The room intact;
The time in order;
And, numbers holding hands with others—

But all of the shirts have been worn,
Their elbows wrinkled, tainted meanwhile
   with the smell of foods
Cooked and left cold.
And, deep in the space between fingers
   hides the sound of the tides.

Yes, at the border, the memories lingering
    at the border are crowded,
Occupying all of the places
    where I tried to be relaxed.
It is when the mirror, oh the mirror, stops me,
That an aspiration is aroused.

The saunter on the carpet. All
The foot prints deposited on the wall paper
    and in the pipes,
All of them, are swept into the Xerox;
I double check that
There is not any cat that has been kicked brutally.

In the room, there are
Always, diagonally,

My eyes only.

An Open Space in the Woods

I frequent this place in the woods,
A place where sunlight seems
   especially concentrated
For no reason or for one that human beings
   will never know.
Somehow, sunlight concentrates
And brightens up this little patch of space. I

Always show up alone,
Yenning
For the loneliness here,
Yet loneliness always shows up in arrays,

Like arrays of trees. Winds and cricket's sound
   were once dismissed here.
And only what was left behind
Would show up here—

But, for the moment, there is nothing here. Me
And myself
Are having a secret rendezvous here.

Agoraphobia

Most of the time, we like to nestle in city.
The window of our crammed little room
Opened only to another tiny window—
As close as the eyes of two persons kissing.

(Although they were mostly shut at the time.)

Wires are intertwined with wires;
Electric appliances,
   surrounded by electric appliances;
Relationships, related by relationships.

Then longing to go out
We go where the sky and the sea
   blend into one color

And wonder upon this one color of

The sea and the sky:

What the hell does this color has to do with us?

The Flower and the Tear and the River

You, extinct already for sure,
Extinguished us both.
I floated among mountains and seas,
    in a posture like a declaration:
The last death of the heaven and the earth.

Inside my body, the flower seasons before death
Did bloom with all their might
    for a thousand times
Equally brilliant, equally brief, equally real.
If you'd asked, well, if
You'd asked for the one thousand and first time,
I would still have made it full bloom,
    with endlessly complex gestures,
Continuing the memory of the last life
In which you had brought the kindles
    and green seedlings.

The seedling grew into me
But you looked in the fire
For the tears that failed to burn down to ashes
And the pains that failed to twist
   and turn into rivers.

You knew about me profoundly,
Except my waiting,
Except how I bloomed as promise.
If I could ask for it, well, if I could,
I would hope this would be the last time I died,
Dead as a seed between cold rock beds,
   undiscovered;
You, like the phantom projected by Time,
Became extinct as I did.

If I could
Reincarnate no more for you,
Let the flower, the tear and the river
   disperse into thin air like phantoms,
Including the writing and reading at this moment.

If I could truly

Treat this as a withering phantom,

And the flower season you missed……

Ode to the Muscle

Sun light shines obliquely on the body of a man,
A sleeping man.

But his muscle is still awake,
As if still guarding him.

In the afternoon, the wind from the sea
Continuously adds into this still-object painting.

On the muscle of the man,
There are touches I left casually.

As I relocate the painting, it hits me:
How fragile does a man need to be

To need to carry all the time such heavy
   and thick muscle?

Between To Love a Person and to Sex a Person

Before the sunlight fully awakes,
I have realized I am in love with someone

Who is far away and yet clear in every details——
Like an animal, I start up abruptly
   from dream, panicked.

I find that the everyday life is a cage;
I need to love, I need to love, love, love.

My finger nails thus become pointed like claws;
My sense of smell, hundred times sharper;

My mane, lustrously smooth; my eyelashes,
   brimming with midnight dews……
For love, I mobilize the entirety of
   my physical body.

My physical body, towards you,
Presses on—beseeches you to respond with yours,

Just and only with
The physical body.

Only on the morning after we have made love
Can we ask nonchalantly each other's name…

Dawn, Dear Dawn, Please Don't Come

On the morning after we made love,
The dawn did not show up as expected.

We groomed in the dark,
Made breakfast.

The commuting crowds cascading from the radio
While we just drank our coffee silently.

Like on a holiday when we wake up early,
The white sheet wrapped up the entire room.

In the dark, we knew the night had gone far away;
In the dark, the bright daylight would never come.

In this undecipherable moment,
Somebody, gently struck upon my body a match on…

The Recipe

Hungry as a bear, I open
A menu of unfathomable profundity, wondering at
Foods spelled out in several languages
Without any verb
But involving certain extremely subtle
Or ephemeral things,
Such as a hand-torn fluffy ball of stuff or
   a three-second dip in water
And a soak in beer, sort of…
However, the rosy rock in a far far away land
   is the theme,
Only available in some seasons
And necessarily harvested after rain
And slowly cooked in barely boiling temperature,
And served in a certain vessel still at a crude stage
To cool down
Which sat through cold nights in cellar

    together with an ancient yeast,
When a certain animal with belly
    almost bursting with spawns or
        more than usually dim-witted—
Then,
Like the Savior, the waiter appears
With a look that he understands it all:
Ready to order?

Meditation

During meditation, I meet
I, a man who only
Lives for training for bigger guns
And no other goals whatsoever.

Gym is the church he visits daily;
Sweating and tearing muscle tissues
    are the ritual of sacrifice;
Soreness and fatigue, the trial.
In the full-length mirror brimming with light,
He catches a glimpse of   God,

Looking down to inspect his own
    blood-charged biceps;
He is a god,
Cursed by gravity—

In front of a long row of dumb bells
    lined up like offerings,
This god is trying hard
To recall

How God is supposed to look like…

Jet Lag

We carry our own individual jet lag
To where we run into each other
—We've met, after all, we've met.

But, I am the crescent moon rising from the sea,
And you, high noon sun;
The rosy clouds that burn in your pupil
   till deep into the night
In turn turn into the setting sun
   that enshrouds my tranquil ascent—

Our bodies are beyond each other's sight.
The exact timing of just missing each other:
   your tonight,
My last? So we can only
Carry the bewilderment that Time
   slips into our luggage,

Continuing our separate journeys home.

Once, as the daytime moon follows my steps, I do
Turn around to confirm, once and again

In your sky,
Constellations are dazzlingly bright all over above.

The Sage on a Toilet

What should a sage think about? What,
When he squads on a toilet,
With the brain and the scorching
   colon equally occupied,
Bloating like a hydrogen balloon:
   "the human body……
The human body, such an undoubtable subjects,
   rich in metaphysical,
     multi-layered symbolism…."
Indeed, the food tempts humans to fall,
Especially the one with thick fibers.
While the toilet is situated in a narrow room,
Its spirit originates from the underground
   sewers of the city.
The sage thinks about all these in admiration:
Lo! Abundant and clear is the spring
   in the toilet. Aye, indeed….

In the mild intoxication of being moved,
The sage smells
What keeps his soul from sublimation:
The 1.5 kilo of the weighty feces.

The Fake Antique

Somehow, I just feel that
The antique is fake. Just like us,
We know our relationship is not "the relationship."

Just like an honest remark
That hoards much falsehood.

Somehow,
Fake antiques just sadden me.

Maybe it is because it can never escape
   the test of Time;
Maybe it is because,
   now displayed under spotlights,

Under all of the attentive eyes,
It bravely speaks the truth.

Animals Come Up To Me

There in the distance, a kangaroo,
Looking up and revealing ivory teeth
   and a pink tongue,
Shockingly like a child who visits
   the dentist alone,
So brave,
Hops up to me.

I do not prepare any food to offer
Except some wicked agenda betrayed
   all over my face;
Even so, a parrot still flies up to me,
A goat trots up to me,
A raccoon sneaks up to me,
And A tortoise and a lizard crawl up to me
Too;

They converse with me through eyes:
Some are tender; some, solemn;
Some, intimate; some, indifferent;

Some talkatively reticent—as if

I also have an animal inside me
Who wanders far away from its cave
   in the morning
Into the air right after rain
Only to realize suddenly the language
   of all beings—

However, I secretly trigger the shutter
And shoot every animal that walks up to me.
The fox, showing up last,
Escapes the massacre.

Just before it turns and vanishes,
We exchange
The most mysterious of our solitude.

The Zoo

An anti-zoo protester like me still
Goes to the zoo, like an member
   of animal protection groups
Protesting against experiments
   with animal in schools and institutes
And enjoying chicken afterwards at home. I
Never looked at rhinoceros in such close distant
And luckily find that they all have double eyelid;
In fact, all animals do—how
Depressing is that; but more desperate is the bird.
If I could ponder in a zoo upon running
Or the issue of hurdle race.
A bird would want to know how,
   to be two hundred meters above the ground,
It would feel like. But, I still walk into the zoo.
Lives are all appallingly been treated as pets.
Amnesiac, losing aggressiveness or curiosity,

    they all stare at the food in my hand,
Including those in the Endangered Zone.
Those are species much more affectionate
    than human beings;
In fact, all other animals are.
Therefore, they are quiet and resigned
    most of the time;
And, human beings flap on the rail
    from time to time
To ask for some of their affection.

Wedding Sleepwalking

Everybody knows I am walking in sleep,
Except myself.

I put up a sober looks and pinch my
Balls, Ouch!, and make sure
   the crotch isn't bulging.

Just as I scoop out the previously hidden
   ring from my pocket,
Someone sends his ring finger right to my face

As if to reprimand me: Wake up!
Instead, he just smiles and thanks—

Before waking up in the morning,
I am back in the bedroom that betrays no evidence,

Like walking through the dark and deep room
   of the ancestry
Into the bridal chamber for the groom.

In a Thick Woods
—On Effigy Mounts

Into the thick woods,
One only sees mushrooms popping out
 from dead trunks of trees,
No wild life at all
Anywhere,

Except the hovering flocks of hawks
 overhead, observing
My head like a mushroom below,

Which can't help shiver a bit.

The Rainbow

The software, *The Present Life,*
Is always busy,

Such as projecting rainbows in the sky—
Whenever the rain
Cools the over-heated engine of the earth

As if
Commanding all creatures to be quiet—
With its own perfection.

Chapter 4 Start

Reading from the Middle

Start Reading from the Middle

Like reading a book from the middle,
I pick a street corner every day and
Start to read—

From the name of the newly acquainted streets
    and road-side venders,
The models of cars and the dishes restaurants offer.
After having read the text on the billboard,
I stand in front of display windows and mumbling:
Discount. The last. Day. ...

Before the night falls maybe,
I have already read the whole section and
Move on to the next chapter. Maybe,

Maybe, I am interrupted in the middle
    by a pedestrian, who says

What another book says:
The rings of Saturn is cutting the earth…
Or, your mother will be, in the next paragraph,
Meeting her lover of the last life
   and give birth to you
In a flood that flows past your hometown—

Then I fall asleep, dozing off between one sentence
And the next.
Some dictions ferment in my stomach,
And some, between my spine and bladder,
Swell or produce thorns.

Sometimes, an elder who frequents my dreams
Will wipe off his features while
   turning over for me
The page to the next. But,
When I wake up, I seem
To wake up at a page I randomly turn to—

Among what is read, what seems to have been read
   and forgotten, and what has not been read,

Like an old town,
There suddenly seems to be a
   wholly new map today,
So I determine to take a
   totally different route home.

I expect to meet a passerby
And recognize him before he me.
But, both putting on the cold politeness
   on the face,
We slightly slow down the pace,

As if one has almost finished a movie before
Realizing having seen it—I
Always start reading from the middle
And keep this completely from him,

Refraining from revealing the slightest trace
   of the antecedent
Or the ending.

The Autumn of New York

From Lexington 59th to Sutton Place
   subway station,
It's a rather long walk.
I imagine how you walk through this passage,
Passing the struggling boutiques on both sides—
Furniture, carpets, massage.
The trees in the little park on the corner
   have all turned brown.
In a town where most people settle there
   for job, you say:
"None of the friends close to my heart
   live in town…,"
And, therefore,
Have become estranged to them eventually; and, I
Don't even live in this country,
   not belonging here. I
Walk on the passage you would

    definitely take every day,
Where the sparrows, squirrels and ravens
    are struggling to survive;
The vendors on roadsides are your brothers,
The granny selling flowers, your mother.
We once celebrated together the opening
    of a new café in the neighborhood;
I ordered the sinfully delicious bagel and latte,
Stood in front of your house, and,
    with the ever changing doorman,
Exchanged goodbye hugs.

Wide Open

Last night, I once tried
To open my body wide as the land did.

In the morning, I woke up
With a funny feeling of being furrowed.

Beyond the window, the weather was lovely
    and the livestock drooped grazing,
And many a sharecropper looked satisfied,

Sauntering around,
Most of whose names I could not even recall…

The Last Grain of Corn in My Dinner Plate

In the dinner plate lies the last grain
    of corn of the winter,
Originally lying in a hungry corn field.
The corn field lies on a yellow earth plateau
    very far from me;
The plateau lies in the arms of the earth;
The earth is held in the hand of nothingness.

Nothingness whispers into my ear:

"As for food, thou shall not overeat…

But must
Finish the very last grain in plate.

The Plant Empire

Once, one plant-ruled empire was
   followed by another—
They had been so quiet,
And almost motionlessly
Ruling.

I, winds, clouds, the sky—
I'd met some trees that exposed the lung to the sky,
Who suffered ages of agony just
To breathe; I never had realized how
The annual rings formed

So introvertly, so slowly,
One circle formed beyond another,
Circling and circling into a solid
Stance.

I wonder how long that agonizing tear
   between an exhale and
An inhale,
Would take—
I could only see things much briefer,
Such as blooming, such as shedding,

Such as mushrooms sprouting
   from the fallen rotten trunks,
Such as weeds spreading over back yards
   and paths.
But, I knew I was heading into
This empire ruled by plants, many of
   whose names I did not know,
Many of whose species I could not tell—

Many of whom were guarding
   a secret center. I knew
They were watching me quietly:
My animal body, animal heart,
Animal soul—
I knew I belonged to things

that lasted much shorter.

Walking past a garden of anonymous plants,
I saw the plants was using branches and leaves
To protect the morning dews with utmost care,
Keeping them so pristine and intact,
Hidden in the depths overlooked by the sunlight.

Indeed, each and every one was an oval diamond
And the diamonds belonged to things
   much briefer than me;
I stepped on the plants,
Feeling how they snapped and fell
   one after another,

Feeling, at the same time,

The resolution
Of guarding the humanity.

84.

And Then I Fell Asleep

And then I fell asleep. I slept between one sentence
And another;
Some dictions fermented in the guts,
Some between the spine and bladder,
Swelling, or growing thorns.

Sometimes, an old man who frequented my dreams
Would smear his features while
Turning the pages for me. But,
I seemed to wake up at
A page randomly turned to—

It was a page either read, or so I thought,
   and forgotten or never been read yet;
The page, like an old city,
Was suddenly mapped fresh new today.
I was determined to take a totally
   different route home.

I expected to meet a pedestrian

And to recognize him before he me
While we kept our cold politeness
And both slowed down our paces,

As if it occurred to me at the end of a movie
That I had seen it—I
Always started reading from the middle
And kept it completely secret from him,

Without revealing even the slightest clue
Or the ending.

Beyond the Window

Mid-autumn in Iowa. Beyond the morning
   window, it was still a bright warm day.
The clouds sauntered;
A line of geese flew by

Straight, neat,
Like a brown airplane,
But more like an arrow

With the will of iron shooting towards
   the magnetic South.

In the afternoon that day, a few sparrows,
   bushwhacking,
Spread like a destroyed troop
Flying north—but in the next second

They might just stop
Like a flock of sticky homeless,
    littered around the city,
Tumbling in the wind, in all directions,
    like trash with brown camouflage…

"The winter is yet to come…,"
    looking out of the window, I wonder:
Be a goose or a sparrow?

The Look

Nowadays, no matter what people do,
They all have to put on a certain look. The maestro
Has a maestro look; the ordinary
Can't help putting on a gangster look—
    last night in gym
I found that everybody, as if in uniform,
All put on the no-bull-shit,
Sweat-spurting gym look:

Compression sweat-wicking tops
    with labeled trainers;
Sports drink with high protein for muscle growth.

Some posed on yoga mattresses
    like a sweating fish,
With twisting posture like a camel
    yearning for mating,

Or earthworm eating dirt angrily,
Or snakes copulating rigorously,
Or quiet scorpions digging a trap pit—

And I
Thought to myself

I was but like a wild kid,
Looking for some place wild to have wild fun in…

Entering

Come in, human beings,
Come in—

This was once the sacred temple
    where gods resided.
Now, it is in ruins,
    incense and candles extinguished,
More like a gym brimming
    with the smell of love making
Or like a Yoga room with chanting lingering
Like the sandal burned the night before.

Swelling blood flowed past membrane;
    nerve cell neurites bulged,
Growing into the many tumors
    that occupied the soul.
Bodies, the ones you have entered,

In the end, turns into a Sanskrit chant fleeting away

Leaving your body behind.
Afterwards, you re-ensemble yourself
Into an expensive theme park,
Erecting roller coaster, shooting up
   towards the navel or anus of the celestial body,
Or plunging into the mouth of gods,
Letting demons devour your guts.
The primitive fire roasts your senses exquisitely.
   Then,

You invite me to enter
Your moist and warm virtual reality.
   Never to be won and possessed
Is the G spot hidden perfectly well;
   you and I, identically,
Attack and attack each other;
Both are verging on the orgasm of vaporization:

"Our bodies are about to enter
   the dusk of The New Era.

The golden gamma cosmic ray
    penetrates the scorching eyeballs...."
The gigantic blindness,
Descending like the eternal night,
Covered, like a gauze of modernism,
The alter where gods have already turned into dust.

At this moment, our bodies still lie together
As if we have used the same a public toilet
    that was deserted too long,
Still obnoxiously stinky.
We are hungry and thirsty,
    with agonizing pain in the guts,
Bringing nothing with us—

And yet still inviting each other
To enter each other;

Enter and enter, again and again...

Measuring Temperature

We stick a dazzling crystal rod
Into a child's anus.
When they grow a little older,
   gaining some strength,
We put it under their armpits instead:
   squeeze tight.
When hair shows up in the armpit,
Smelling funny as it sweats regularly,
We put the rod in their mouth,
Tugging it under the tongue
For three minutes.

Then, the rod disappears;
Someone points a small pistol,

Straight at my ear

The Wound

You had no idea what your body had told me.
Afterwards, I still recognized you,
Though, that day, your expression, hair,
And clothes
Were curiously silent—but

At that moment, I pressed my ear
   close to your under belly,
Like listening to the fetus's heartbeat;
In fact,
I wanted to hear the heartbeat earlier

Than the fetus, the zygote,
And the arousal of desire. But you,
Wounded all over, stood up
And left my room with wounds everywhere,
   pushing through the dumb door,

Walking into this city that was wounded all over,

Like a man whose soul were decorated
   all over with various kinds of medals:
"The scabs and scars invisible to the mortal…"
I said. I recognized you

Because of those,
We recognized each other.

Plastic Flowers

For these, I cannot forgive the human being.

Yesterday, as I sauntered in the cemetery,
There offered in front of the deceased's name
   on white marble
Were plastic flowers,

Whitish,
Drooping in sadness,

Like ghosts trapped in the mortal world:
"Have you seen how the plastic flowers
   look like when they whither?"

In comparison with the long-lasting,
   the rest just looks stale and old—
And the human being will eventually

Be gone a moment earlier.

Will of the Fallen Leaves

Do you think Autumn arrives here by chance? Just
Stopping over casually?
And becoming a quiet companion by your side?

In fact, none of the fallen leaves
   stop over by chance;
They all have vowed to fall
On the spot where they are lying now—

Like tattoos on the earth,
That seem to float randomly
   on to your chest or gluteal cleft,
As concentrated as needle points

In the form of pain,
Their will
Fights against time—when the wind starts to blow,

Sweeping away all of the withered
    and the decayed,
We, each of us, were left lying where
We are lying now.

Chapter 5 Thoughts On Poetry (selected)

1.

But, poetry, the written poetry, is always just a corpse, from which the breath has left; it is just a map entitled "Utopia,"

Or a mundane foreign land that one will never reach; always just one of the most trustworthy blueprints of the Never Never Land.

The true poetry exists only in the moment when it is finished: while the fuzzy atmosphere of the uncertain circumference of reality starts to flow, it stays dead still like the shady movement a spirit projects onto the wall, like the aurora brushes across arctic sky, like a quiet flute charged with imagery by imagination.

2.

About poetry, I can't help quote Rilke: "I have no theory. Why should I have one?"

3.

Lightning flashes across the sky, shooting several cold, mechanic shafts of white light through the window. I count silently: one, two, three, four, ... until the thunders beat on my eardrum. The larger the number, the farther away the lightning.

One, two, three, four, five, six,... Once, I just kept on counting and the thunder never came.

I was sure that there would be thunders,

And the moment a thunder was heard, a poem was born ... though all I could do was to go on counting.

4.

Zhuang Zi once told a story about a shadow and the shadow of its shadow (or wangliang).

Wanglinag, tired of always dancing the exact steps which the shadow did, complained about it to the shadow. The shadow could only apologize for it, explaining that it too could only always dance the exact steps of suosi (literally, "the one it serves," or the form).

And, the form cannot be its own master—therefore, "the form and the shadow walk in perfect unison"; above levels and levels of "resigned involuntariness," the ultimate master is what Zhuang Zi called "zhenjun" (literally, the true lord).

Zhenjun is like the true heart, the life, the true temperament, the soul of a person.

And poetry, therefore, is the dialogue between wangliang and zhenjun when they encounter.

5.

All languages start in the state of roaming.

The prose roams in daytime streets and lanes; the fiction, in the labyrinth theater of the reality; poetry, rather, wanders in a dream land, in mirage—however, the distance to the path leading back to the homeland is, paradoxically, closer.

6.

Poet Yan Li said, "There is an Eighth Day in the calendar week of a poet." On the day, the human beings can "rest beyond time, savoring the superfluous."

Indeed, poetry is superfluous. See how the ants live—not a single second is superfluous.

7.

Hemingway said, "Stop when you feel the impulse to write."

This seems to be a torturing regimen for a poet, as if a gastronome takes part in a fasting diet—and for what? Trying to sense any taste out of pure fresh water?

The impulse of creating may be worth grabbing, but as I grow more "experienced' in writing poetry, I seem to be more able to realize the true value and beauty of spontaneity.

When a poet can compose poetry to a level where he freely write or not write, what kind of level of poetic Samadhi would that be?

8.

I always felt an urge to escape whenever I lectured any courses related to poetry, or an urge to stay firmly put to cut myself open, displaying any possible mechanism of the birth of poetry—but there was none, in fact. Just as breaking a toaster apart, one would not find its soul, or "the God of the toaster," even less likely a well toasted piece of bread.

What braced me along to be able to walk into a lecture on poetry was courage merely and courage had nothing to do with poetry. More often than not, the reason was that I was afraid that other teachers might ruin the class. That's all.

There are worse poetry teacher than I.

In desperation, I vaguely realized that poetry could only come from poetry and returned to poetry.

"Laying down the textbook and leaving the classroom, we might reunite in the land of poetry someday,"

Said I when I dismissed the class.

9.

"Poetry happens where prose ends and disappears," said someone.

Where all prose ends, the summer bugs smell the ice and deserts dream of the ocean. However, poetry does not necessarily happen. It is silly to liaise poetry with prose in the first place.

Grape juice and wine should not sit on the same shelf.

"At least neither can exist without language…," some may say.

But, prose reaches a little lower than language while poetry a little higher.

10.

The discipline of poetry. Yes, the composition of poetry requires the poet to be disciplined in the strictest standard.

The heart of poetry must stay alert all the time, both day and night.

Practice, practice and practice more.

Listen to the thunder of poetry where there is none. Then lift tons like grams and move the immensely weighty universe with a mere few words.

Feel no pity discarding any material of non-poetic genre. Prose has its own path; fiction, its own bridge. The temperament decides the contents; the contents, the form. Composing poetry is the process of discovering inwardly one's own self. The regimen of composing poetry is like military training or spiritual pursuit. Nothing can be achieved with any exertion "less than the utmost one."

Be brave to struggle forward. Be forever relentless in the sweet solitude.

It is acceptable to produce poor poetry; but dishonest ones, never! Prematurity is not a sin. The success of revolution is always somewhere beyond reach.

Be dedicated: the first and the last principle.

11.

Passing by an exquisitely decorated pet supply store on Tianmu North Road, I saw a line of poetry by some poet no longer around, posted on the window pane Roughly this:

Every pearl started out as a grain of sand, so is love.

I started at the glance of it—first of all, there should be a line of poetry on the window pane (and no one buy poetry in bookstore?):

Secondly, there is hardly any relation possible between this poem and pet-keeping. (How many pet-owner relationship starts with the former being a pain to the latter?)

Thirdly, something is rather seriously wrong here for it involves the cognition of the nature of love.

To me, love is love, pearl pearl, and sand sand—

an iron rod can be whetted down into a needle for embroidery but never a chunk of brick, just as stated in the famous Zen koan.

If it is love, really love, the true love, how can it be treated as something else in the moment when it happened? Unless it was something else from the very beginning.

Gold can be refined and diamond, polished—love, likewise can be learned and epiphanized—but, intrinsically, love is love, never the product of transformation. Millennia of the alchemy have proven that gold cannot be produced from processing lead or mercury.

For a line of poetry that I could not bring myself to agree with, every time I passed by Tianmu North Road ever since, I could not help becoming grumpy.

12.

Years ago, I once joined a screenwriting course to learn how to write a play. The instructor brought up an iron rule: A play can accommodate only one "coincidence." More than that, the play'd be crushed. Keeping that in mind, I deliberated the point and recalled the plots of all the movies I'd seen and found it WAS so. How about poetry? Is there one iron rule for composing poetry? I always hoped there was but also there was none.

If yes, poetry would be easy to teach; there'd be Dummy's Guide for Writing Poetry; if no, we can have more fun with poetry and develop more of ourselves.

As written in The Diamond Sutra: What is an iron rule is exactly not one, which is the iron rule.

This is the highest level one can get in composing poetry.

13.

Is there literature in Heaven? Never heard so.

Probably no poetry either.

To those outside the Pearl Gate, to live in the heaven would feel like a poem, but those inside it do not need it. Originally, poetry was written for human beings living in the purgatory.

After deliberation, all poetic imagery, such as the Yellow Spring and the Emerald Sky, reeks with ambience of the Hell.

The poet Tu Fu was like a Lucifer that fell into the mundane world, in whose mind that might be muddled with the red dust there was still glimpses of the Heaven left, with which he chanted poetry to the dim and dumb human beings.

In the end, this Lucifer, who was unable to find his way back to the Heaven, constructed a heaven of his own in the mundane world. Of course, we thought it was Hell all along.

Because only the Hell can produce poetry, poets and those who truly moved by poetry.

14.

Hegel, the German philosopher, said, "there have to be some people in a nation who watch the sky so that there'd be hope; if all of the people in a nation are concerned with only what happens down where they stand, there'd be no future for them."

Those who watch the sky, as mentioned here, are poets.

There is no compliment to poets more solemn than Hegel's.

15.

Should poetry be "readable to grannies and children even"?

In a Buddhist Script, there is a line reads: "Buddha speaks in one tone, and all beings understand it as its kind would."

Whether this understanding is based on what kind this person belongs to or on the true original intention of the Buddha?

Does "One Tone" resemble something like the origin of everything in the Universe? The sound of a one-palm clap? Sanskrit? Or "Om"?

I cannot compose a poem like Bai Juyi who included the "grannies" and "children" into his readership. I can only put down my own "One Tone," writing what I can stand to read, not concerned about if others can understand it or how they might interpret it.

16.

Once in a lecture, I blurted out, "The greatest enemy of literature is a concept." I regretted it immediately, for I very well realized that running along deeper into this subject the speech would end in extremely abstract monologue of argument and fell into another "concept."

As an old saying goes, the temperament decides the contents and the contents, the form. The worst of worst scenarios was to do the opposite. Working against the inclination, I produced teams of works which were forced, duplicated, patched-up and more form than quality. The poetry, or the Pure Infant, was tortured and became "an oracle poem," in which one could find an answer to everything, from wedding, funeral to all occasions.

The less worse scenario is to cut in from the contents. Predetermined "contents" are the concept itself. Why not go along with your innate temperament to discern, to feel and to write? In other words, admitting that every soul is unique.

As a western novelist once said, "in literature, why not let all and everything emits its own light? The thinner the artificial polishing the better, or it'd become a light pollution, blocking stars light years away.

Recently, I have read in the diary of a Hinayana cultivator a line which says: "when ordinary people think "what is this?" they are actually thinking over a concept and when a Zen thinker think "what is this?" he is really thinking about its "nature."

The nature is where the poetry lies.

17.

I always feel that it is very hard to explain what poetry is to poets; either ending easily in forced ideas or, literally, in a dead end. Lifelessly boring, diminishing the capacity and possibility of poetry, in fact. It can very rightly be blamed on the way they teach poetry in the present education system.

The other day, I spotted a poem called "The Introduction to Poetry" in a column, "Poem of the Day," in the newsletter of Poetry Foundation, which deals with exactly what worries me. I just have to share it with you, "introduction to poetry" by Billy Collins:

I ask them to take a poem
and hold it up to the light
like a color slide
or press an ear against its hive.

*I say drop a mouse into a poem
and watch him probe his way out,*

*or walk inside the poem's room
and feel the walls for a light switch.*

*I want them to waterski
across the surface of a poem
waving at the author's name on the shore.*

*But all they want to do
is tie the poem to a chair with rope
and torture a confession out of it.*

*They begin beating it with a hose
to find out what it really means.*

Do we really need to torture a modern poem to "understand" it?

18.

I once lived in the North America for three years, leaving Chinese behind completely, and studying hard in courses on English poetry, and trying, just as what Eileen Chang said, to grow a tree with the seed blown across over there. The teachers included elegant retired old ladies, young boys moonlighting in cram schools, and young female literati with flowing long hair.

They were all passionate in teaching but seemed to keep a distance somehow from "poetry."

I finally gave up any attempt to compose poetry in English.

An unexpected reward was that I was a better writer of English medical science papers.

Reminiscing on this unfulfilled dream, I ran into Van Gogh.

To conclude Van Gogh's paintings in one remark: "Sunlight" is rediscovered in the oils.

And I see sunlight only in Chinese, not in English.

19.

The nightmare of a poet: you wake up one day to find that all that you have written have become cliché.

And then, you also find that all of the poetry composed by other poets, from "Before the bed, the moon shines bright" to "Under the same bright moon," all of them becomes cliché.

Mine included, from inside the mind to inside the mouth, whatever can be said and written is re-saying what other human beings have said and thought.

Just as the digital camera "liberates" photography, the general education "liberates" literary writing and the internet and 3C products "liberates" broadcasting and duplicating. The other side of liberation is endless vulgarization, secularization and deprivation of individuality.

This forms a seamless era loop which there is no interrupting or terminating—from cliché breeds more clichés. Generations after generations, too vast a clan to identify any member.

And, what's worse, a value forms: only cliché can express sincere compliment, only cliché.

20.

A Turkish visiting poet put down on the notebook in my hand a mysterious number: 300.

He told me in heavily accented English: 300 copies, that is.

The number of copies sold of a poetry collection by poets all over the world, no matter whether the famous or the anonymous: 300 copies. We all stared at this unbelievable number and could not help let a hearty smile escape us. I responded without thinking: In the Taiwanese expression, there are more poets than poetry readers.

Therefore, it is highly possible that many of these 300 copies were bought by the poet himself.

"Globally speaking, it is probably in China only that poetry can achieve a sale more than 5000 copies," I said, for a friend of mine published his poetry in Beijing and the first print was 5000 copies.

Huge population means more readers, and therefore higher loyalty to poetry.

Mainland China today is a fantasy dreamland of modern poetry.

21.

I remember I received a letter from a reader years ago, whose contents I have forgotten completely. What I can recall of it now is the little message left on the lid of the envelope: I shout at the top of my lung so that I can hear the echo.

This message left me pondering.

About the mountain in front of the poet.

Shapeless and formless, there is no way to tell how high and far it is. Only when the poet roars so hard as if he is going to explode can its existence be heard—for there would be echoes.

With the echoes, one hears the mountain.

With the echoes, one can tell the existence, the figure, the expression and the truth of the mountain.

22.

Poets are creatures living afloat in the echoes.

Every poem is a shout a poet makes with all his might, investing the whole of his life and facing its truth. When the sound dies, he dies with it.

As for the mountain in front of him,

It takes a mountain that is high and wide enough to produce echoes that are resonant, otherworldly and distinct enough.

There is only one catch here: what if the mountain does not exist?

www.ingramcontent.com/pod-product-compliance
Lightning Source LLC
Chambersburg PA
CBHW020411080526
44584CB00014B/1277